Pathways

A self-help guide for families when
Searching for placement in a group home.

Theresa Loretta Gabriel

Copyright – 2014
Publisher – Theresa Loretta Gabriel
Lancaster, PA
Printed in the United States of America
ISBN 139781499628456
Registered with the Library of Congress

Edited by Marguerite Peters and Monica Pattern

This book is dedicated to my Aunt Loretta, whose belief in me never faulted. She has always been a source of inspiration for me. Her continued encouragement for me to be who I wanted to be helped become who I am today.

It is also dedicated to all the individuals who have forever changed my life. It has been a privilege to care for and love them and have them love me back
unconditionally throughout the years.

A special thank you to everyone who helped me put this guide together. I hope it is a resource that you will use often and learn from. I know putting it together with the help of family and friends reminded me that we would not exist without the love and support of others.

Please note the author has changed the names of all those mentioned in this guide to provide anonymity.

Table of Contents

Introduction

I began my career in human services as a housekeeper and cook in an Intermediate Care Facility (ICF) in New York. It was here that I found my calling to work in human services. I fell in love with the individuals I worked with, especially the clients. Simply put, I loved my job. From the moment I first entered my first ICF, it took only a few weeks to realize this was what I wanted to do with my life.

In the late 1980's I relocated to Pennsylvania. It had always been my parent's plan to retire and move to Pennsylvania. When their move was imminent, I relocated to Pennsylvania as well. Two weeks before my parents were to move to Pennsylvania my father passed away from cancer. His dream of retiring to Pennsylvania would live on through my mother. It was all the more important to me now to make my new life in Pennsylvania a success and something that not only would my mother, my children be proud of, but something I would be proud of myself.

Soon after moving to Pennsylvania, I wanted to return to work. I soon learned that Pennsylvania was different than New York in that they do not have ICF Units. Instead they have *group* homes. Over the next 19 years, I worked in various group homes living my life's calling.

This guide will help families find the right placement home for their loved one. Please note that some of the information in this guide will vary from State to State. Additionally, State and Local agencies, non-profit organizations may also have different policies and procedures.

Chapter One

A Look into the Author's Life

I was born into a New York, Italian-Catholic family. This tells you that I know commitment, loyalty, rules, and most of all family. My parents, Eileen and Peter, never missed a day's work their whole adult life. They instilled in each of their children a sense of responsibility and commitment. I am the second of five children and all five of us lead very different and productive lives. But, no matter where we are (from New York to Texas), we will always be family.

My early adult life was trying to find my niche; where did I belong? I dabbled in catering, acting, and a cleaning service; just to name a few. Nothing ever lasted, but all those experiences certainly did make for very well-rounded life.

My career in human services started with a well-known ICF (Intermediate **C**are **F**acility) home organization in New York. When I first reported to the ICF I was excited and nervous. I prayed I would fit in with everybody. I felt like a new door was opening for me, and when I walked through this door I had such an overwhelming desire to make this my niche, my calling.

I was fortunate that my previous experience in house cleaning was an asset as I started my new career in ICF. House cleaning isn't always about "cleaning" but the nuance of creating a "house" into a "home" and this came to serve me well.

One of my attributes is cooking. Being in an Italian family we cook, we eat! I remember though there was always a competitiveness amongst the children for who made the best pot of sauce {marinara}. Whose pot of sauce would be better than my father's. To this day I think we each came close but never quite as good as my father's, and perhaps that is as it should be. So, preparing meals for the individuals in the ICF was truly a joy for me. It was cooking for my other family without all the who can top dad's pot of sauce.

However, I really had no experience in caring for people with disabilities. This was going to be out of my comfort zone, but the individuals with whom I would care for made me want to step out of my comfort zone and learn what it takes to care for people with disabilities.

This is my story sharing some of my experiences, the good, the bad, and the sad over the nearly 20 years in the human services. My experiences are just that-they are my experiences. We will all have different experiences whether it be giving care or receiving care, but in the end those experiences mold who we become, who we are as a person.

I remember pulling into a large circular driveway. The house was beautiful. It was well-maintained with beautiful bushes, trees, and flower beds with vibrant colors and wonderful thick green moss. A warm, comforting feeling came over me just standing in the driveway. I rang the doorbell, but no one came to the door. Turning the knob, I discovered it was unlocked. I stepped inside, scanned the room and it was absolutely lovely. Beautifully decorated with all the comforts of home and it was very well-kept.

It was quiet in the house, and I began wondering where everyone was. Deep in my thoughts, I got startled when I heard, "Hello, you must be Theresa, I'm Daisy, the supervisor; everyone is at their day program." We shook hands and the warmth of Daisy's personality came through in her handshake.

Daisy gave me a tour of the home (ICF) that had many bedrooms; in fact this was the home to 13 clients. There was a nurse, several direct care workers, and overnight staff. An apartment was attached to the ICF for the assistant manager. The ICF would always be staffed 24/7.

My responsibilities were to maintain the cleanliness of the home, food shopping, and preparing of all meals. There were little tricks of the trade that were shared with me. For example, I realized everyone always had prune juice in the morning. I was told this helped to keep them "regular" with their bowel movements, thus eliminating the need for stool softener. This would also mean the clients would be able to take one less medication. These tricks of the trade came to serve me well and increased my depth of knowledge in the care of these 13 clients.

I spent a good deal of time in the kitchen. It was large and beautiful; more than I could ever imagine having on my own. It had kitchen gadgets I never knew existed. Early on, I found the Good Housekeeping Cookbook in the kitchen and this soon became my bible of cooking.

It didn't take long to develop close friendships with all the staff and my supervisor, Daisy. People in healthcare are typically very giving, caring, thoughtful people. My close friendships with everyone blossomed into a second family for me.

The clients of this ICF had various disabilities. They were all friendly and loving people, and I instantly became friends with all of them.

One day I was preparing lasagna for dinner and one of the more curious clients, John, wondered into the kitchen to see what I was cooking and asked if he could help. I was so excited that he took such an interest, and it was a meal I'll never forget. Together we prepared the lasagna, building layer upon layer of lasagna, but soon I would learn that we were building a friendship at the same time. It was so easy to see that he was so thrilled to be in the kitchen; almost like it was forbidden.

Well, turns out it was forbidden. Our time came to halt when Daisy walked into the kitchen and saw the two of us making lasagna. Daisy pulled me aside and informed me that clients were not allowed in the kitchen. I couldn't believe it-not allowed in the kitchen-this is their home and the kitchen is a part of their home. This really bothered me, because I could see John's excitement in doing something that many of us would probably see as a chore. I decided I was going to talk to Daisy about this policy and find out why. Of course, I had to admit it could very well be for their personal safety.

I had a lot of respect for Daisy, and I felt that she was someone I could approach and discuss this openly. So, the next day I went to talk with her and I simply asked why? She looked surprised by my question. She admitted that nobody ever asked why the clients couldn't be in the kitchen and more surprising no one ever cooked with them before. Daisy looked around the room where we were having this discussion, almost as if she was searching for an answer, but there wasn't one. Daisy could see the excitement I saw in John when we making the lasagna; she knew he was having a great time. So, together Daisy and I worked on a schedule that would allow all interested and capable clients to help in the kitchen.

I share this story with you so you know that if you discover an interest, a hobby, that someone truly enjoys but policy would otherwise prevent them from enjoying it-don't give up. Talk about it, set up perimeters, supervise and always reassess periodically to make sure it is working. This story just reminds me that it is the simple things in life can make people happy and sometimes we just forget that. So, make a tray of lasagna with someone special, and as you layer each layer ever so carefully, take a moment to appreciate the friendship you are building.

There is one more story I would like to share with you that I know changed the lives of those I love and cared for.

Christmas was approaching and truth be told I love Christmas. I love the whole season of Christmas. The ICF house was decorated with a beautiful tree and lights all about the house. Many of the clients had family who had called to say they would be there to visit their loved one on Christmas Day. However, sadly two of our clients had no family. I could see that sadness in their face of not having anyone to share all this Christmas beauty, the Christmas spirit with.

I was excited about Christmas. I was scheduled to be off and my family would all be coming to my home for Christmas. However, despite all my excitement there was a cloud just hovering over me. I couldn't shake the sadness I was feeling for the two clients that had no family. Family is family whether it is blood family or those we invite into our lives. So, I thought what is another two more people.

When I went to work the next day I went straight to Daisy's office to ask her about inviting the two clients to my family Christmas dinner. I was so nervous-I mean cooking in the kitchen with our clients was one thing but it is another thing to take them out of their environment into a new environment, totally outside the ICF. But, setting my nerves aside, I went into Daisy's office and just blurted out, "I would like to take Mark and June home for Christmas dinner."

Mark was a middle-aged man who lived with Down's Syndrome. He was kind and gentle. June was middle-aged and full of life. She was funny and had a wonderful personality. She never complained that her body was confined to a wheelchair due to cerebral palsy.

Daisy looked up from her desk and the look on her face was nothing short of puzzlement. She slumped back in her chair and stretched her arms over her head. She began to rotate her head back and forth, up and down, and then side to side. It looked like she was trying to get the pain out of her neck; I was hoping that pain in her neck wasn't me. I stood there anxiously awaiting her answer, and finally the words came out, "Well, I see no reason why they shouldn't go – it's Christmas." I couldn't believe my ears! I couldn't wait to tell Mark and June. The excitement in their faces was like the excitement on the 4th of July when fireworks burst into bright sprinkles of reds, blues, green, and whites. It would be Christmas for all of my families.

Driving home that afternoon I thought to myself this is going to be the best Christmas ever. I was planning all the meals in my head, what we would have dessert, setting the table, etc. and I was just so excited. This would be the first time my family would be meeting my new friends and seeing first-hand this new life I have. Not only would be young son and daughter be meeting my new friends, my parents, my siblings would be seeing this whole new side of me. Something that I knew it my heart would not be a short-term job; I wanted them to see I had found my calling. I was caught up in the prospect of my dream Christmas that OH MY GOODNESS, like a bolt of lightning, I snapped to and realized I had a problem with my wonderful Christmas plan; I had no ramp for getting June up the two flights of stairs to my apartment.

I had to stay focused and think rationally. I wasn't going to let anything keep my family from meeting my friends; everything will work out. My dad can build anything. As soon as I got home, I couldn't wait to call my dad and tell him my plans, how two of my new friends would be joining our family for Christmas dinner. I rambled on and on in all my excitement, talking about the ramp, work, family coming over-who knows what I said. When I finally s topped rambling, my father in his patriarch way said, "I'm sorry Theresa, but if you invite those people, I won't be there. I can't be around people like that." I was shocked. Keep in mind my family has never really met anyone with a disability, so this would be totally new experience and something clearly out of their comfort zone. I failed to keep this in mind. I paused for a few minutes, totally at a loss for words. His attitude shocked me. Then finally I mustered up the courage to say, "I'm sorry to hear to hear that Dad." We will miss you not being here for Christmas" and then I hung up the phone. I cried for hours.

After my crying spell, I was trying to figure out what I was going to do. Does my second family get hurt in the process of being with my first family? I knew in my heart there was no way I could tell June and Mark they couldn't come for Christmas dinner. I was sipping on a cup of tea, deep in thought over my dilemma, when suddenly I hear this banging. Then I start hearing voices and quite a ruckus coming from my front yard. I set down my cup of tea and looked out the front window. There was my Dad, along with a friend, carrying plywood from the back of his truck and a hammer hanging from his belt. They were building the ramp! The love I felt for my dad just rushed through my heart and put the biggest smile on my face and tears of joy in my eyes. I was so proud of him...this is who we are. We are family. It didn't even matter to me what changed his mind, only that he did. My family arrived on Christmas Day and my first family met my second family and the spirit of Christmas filled my home with love. We planned for more future activities together. This was my gift of Christmas.

The moral of this story is we all learned something that day. June and Mark learned that employee's can be more than staff. They can develop friendships and know there are people who really do care about them. June and Mark began opening up more to other staff and trusting people more. Of course, employees will always come in go into the lives of our clients, but without opening our hearts and taking risks we will never have the chance to form friendships that will change our lives for the better.

When I relocated to Pennsylvania, I promised my friends at the New York ICF home that I would remain close no matter what the distance. I wrote letters, sharing stories of my new life in Pennsylvania. I learned that June developed strong friendships with the staff at the home. Mark had passed away shortly after I left New York. When I thought about Mark's passing, I knew in my heart he carried home with him the love of this Christmas past.

My family learned that people with disabilities are people just like us. They have personalities and feelings. It took only a short time for the families to blend and become one big Italian and not so Italian family.

My own lesson from this was a discovery about myself. I learned without realizing it at first that I was born to be an advocate for those who can't speak up for their own well-being. I was the voice for many who didn't have one. I spoke up when I felt policy needed to be challenged or if a client's rights weren't being honored. It is important that if you feel something isn't right to speak up. Share your concerns with management. Remember everyone has rights and you may need to be their voice!

Once you have made the decision that it is time to find placement for your loved one, you want to have peace of mind that you have found a home where your loved one will be happy and receive excellent care. Below is a list of resources that can help you begin your journey.

Resources pulled from:

http://www.apha.org/about/Public+Health+Links/LinksGovernment HealthAgencies.htm

Health Resources and Services Administration

The Health Resources and Services Administration (HRSA), is the primary Federal agency for improving access to health care services for people who are uninsured, isolated or medically vulnerable.www.hrsa.gov

Centers for Medicare and Medicaid Services

Centers for Medicare and Medicaid Services (CMS) aims to ensure effective, up-to-date health care coverage and to promote quality care for beneficiarieswww.cms.hhs.gov

Agency for Health Care Research and Quality

The mission of the Agency for Health Care Research and Quality (AHRQ) is to improve the quality, safety, efficiency, and effectiveness of health care for all. Americans. www.ahrq.gov/

Resources for Autism

National Autism Association
http://nationalautismassociation.org/?gclid=CjwKEAjw9-CfBRD8lt_w86zJiDUSJAADZA38-aRxd-8kp8v_55NxqMv4FjUloqw91L0zM6vIjri8WhoCoYrw_wcB

Autism Speaks
http://www.autismspeaks.org/family-services/community-connections/financial-assistance

Youth Services

SAMHSA - Substance Abuse and Mental Health Services Administration
http://findtreatment.samhsa.gov/locator/link-focChild

Mental Health

Association for Retarded Citizens
http://www.thearc.org/who-we-are?utm_expid=13574319-4.6lqSc7-ETH6PeZi3JtAvLA.0&utm_referrer=http%3A%2F%2Fwww.thearc.org%2Fwho-we-are%2Fhistory%2Fsegal-account

Government Resources

Department of Health and Human Services
http://www.hhs.gov/

http://www.usa.gov/

To find your state local Social Service Agency
http://healthfinder.gov/FindServices/SearchOrgType.aspx?OrgTy
peID=8

Schools will also provide social workers, psychiatrists and parent groups. It may also be a good idea to put all of the individual's important information in a folder.

Important documents to save in the folder:

- Copy of Birth Certificate
- Copy of Social Security Card
- Security Income and Social Security Assistance (SSI/SSA) Certificate
- Health Insurance Cards
- Medical Records – Remember your rights.
    - http://www.hhs.gov/ocr/privacy/
- School records
- Burial information
- Detailed information on any behavioral issues

Chapter 3– Mission Statements and Documents

Mission Statement

Most organizations will have a Mission Statement. It states their purpose and usually their core values. Some Mission Statements will include a Pledge of Dedication to the individuals they serve. This is their vision of a promise of well-being and commitment to the individuals they serve.

If they have a Mission Statement, ask to read it and request a copy for your records. Having several Mission Statements from a variety of organizations will help give you insight into their goals for the individuals they serve. Is their mission one of servitude or integrating your loved one into society? Find the mission that will bring you peace of mind in knowing your loved one will be looked after with all the love and support they need away from home.

Documents

Every individual who finds placement in a group home has rights. There are several documents that are signed by the individual and updated annually.

These documents are the Bill of Rights, Civil Rights and Right of Privacy. You should request copies of these documents as well. They may come in handy if any type of problem with their placement develops. It would benefit you further if these documents are signed by the individual and an employee.

Individual Support Plan (ISP)

Simply explained, an ISP is a document that maps out the individual's progress, goals, concerns, wishes, and behavioral problems if they exist. This should be done annually in a meeting with all directly involved in the care of your loved one.

The ISP is written by the staff, treatment specialists, work coach, or day program employee all of whom attend this meeting with the individual. It is good if you can attend the meeting too. If you are unable to attend, you should request a copy of the ISP.

Should you have any questions on the ISP, do not hesitate to contact the supervisor of the home in which you loved one has been placed. Write your questions down ahead of time so you stay on task.

Chapter 4 – Your Guided Tour of Homes

In many cases, management has a "select" group of homes they will call upon for a family walk-through. These would be the homes that are well-maintained, inside and out. They may also choose homes that are low-keyed. Low-keyed homes are the ones where the individuals who live there are quiet or do not have sudden outbursts. They would be individuals who typically do not require as much attention as those with more needs.

Next, is something I call, *Curb Appeal.* Group Homes are generally located in residential communities. When you arrive at the home you will be touring, your first impression will be the outside of the home. Is the landscaping nice? Does it look well-maintained? Who maintains the property? Do the clients participate in the upkeep? Can the client help; maybe plant flowers? Or, is an outside company hired? Is there trash and un-kept items in the yard? What about the winter? Is the driveway steep? Who is responsible for snow removal? The staff or is someone hired?

What are the rest of the homes in the neighborhood like? Look at everything! Is this a safe neighborhood? You can always call the local police department and ask for a crime report of that neighborhood. Try and speak with a couple of the neighbors.

When visiting and touring the home, you should ask if this is the home of possible placement for your loved one. You may or may not get a direct answer. You may consider asking a more open-ended question such as, "What is the likelihood or percentage of placement that my loved one will be in this home?" My past experience tells me you probably won't get a direct answer. There are many factors that go into the decision of placement not only on your end, but the organization's end as well. In light of this, be sure to see as many homes as possible. Don't hesitate to go back and revisit those homes that are your top choices.

Once you have found a group home placement for your loved one, it is important to try and visit whenever possible. Vary the day and time of your visits. This will help you know that your loved one is being well cared for at all times. Should you have questions or concerns express them to the staff, and if necessary, the management. It is also important to vocalize to the staff how happy you are with the care your loved one has been receiving. Working in a group home is not always easy and can be far from glamorous, so let them know that you appreciate the care they give your loved one. Just a few words of kindness go a long way.

Now, let's say your loved one has lived happily in a particular home for several years and for some unknown reason, you are informed that they will be moved to another home. I have seen this happen on several occasions. There are group homes where the individuals who live there among the staff have truly become family. If so, such a move for your loved one could be devastating and confusing to them. It could bring out old negative behaviors or even depression. It could also create new behaviors.

Some individuals will not understand why they have been moved. If you feel this move is not in the best interest of your family member, you have the right to speak for them. You *should* speak for them. This is where copies of their Civil Rights and Bill of Rights will come into play. However, on occasion, an individual can be moved without a family's knowledge. In this type of situation, there is very little a family member can do, unless you are prepared to look for other possible placements or bring your loved one into your home. Should this situation happen, visit your loved one as often possible, and try and be positive about the change (i.e. opportunity to make new friends, different social activities this home may have). Change is always difficult, but we have to remember that change can also be good.

There are times when a client is moved for a positive reason. A client's productivity could be enhanced in a different home with clients that are more compatible with his/her attributes. However, sometimes those positive reasons are due to negative actions at the former home. That might mean abusive encounters with another client. Something like this goes back to your visiting as often as possible and not being afraid to ask questions. If you see something not right, like a bruise, or a new behavior pattern, ask about it. Keeping in touch and being well-informed is crucial. If you can't visit as often as you would like, you can always call. When you call, take a few moments and speak with the caregiver. Ask about how your loved one is doing, what activities have then been doing, are they interacting with other clients, eating well. And, don't forget to say a few words of kindness.

Chapter Five – Home Safety: What to Look for in Homes and Questions You Are Entitled to Ask

When families are shown a home as discussed in Chapter 4, they of course take in a home's physical appearance. How it is furnished? What is the décor like? Does the home have a good feeling and comfortable atmosphere? These are definitely important factors, but let's talk about concerns and safety within the home.

If the home has a basement, ask to see it. You want to make sure that it is free of mold and does not have a musty smell. Make sure you ask the staff what the basement is used for. I once worked in a home where the staff's office and small bedroom for overnight staff were located in the basement. One individual had a hobby room despite the mold that was growing there. What was the management's solution? Cleaning it with bleach, but this is only a temporary solution. Mold is a very serious problem, one you should definitely watch out for when touring a home. Mold can appear as green or black spotty patches; usually where moisture can develop (i.e. air conditioning units, bathrooms, sinks (under the sink cabinets; storage closets). High humidity can also increase the likelihood of mold growing.

You also have the right to ask if the home's electricity is up to code. Some of the homes could be older and have old wiring that could pose a danger. How old is the house? How many floors? Does the home have carbon monoxide alerts? Every home should have smoke detectors.

It is required monthly procedure to have a fire drill. What is the evacuation plan? Common practice is to have the clients meet in a designated place outside of the home.

Some homes have a "sleep" staff as well as an "awake" overnight staff. This is done because in most cases it would take two staff members to evacuate the home getting everyone to their designated meeting place. However, in some homes, there is only one staff member responsible during the night either awake or asleep. During the fire drills, staff should get all of the clients out of the home in less than two minutes.

I once worked in a home with a client who had Down's Syndrome and it could be difficult to wake this client. In the same home, there was non-verbal client who needed to be assisted out of bed and walking to the designated place outside. Another individual had Cerebral Palsy who needed a wheelchair. I remember being told we could place her in a blanket and drag her out of the home. I thought really? Employees expressed concern about this plan and suggested a fire exit be put in that client's bedroom. Since the bedrooms were all down one short hallway close together, our suggestion was to knock out part of the wall where there was window and put in a door with a ramp so that staff could get everyone to safety with an additional exit. As staff, we came to learn that it is always better to present an issue or concern with a possible solution. This is something that applies to all families members as well. You should always feel comfortable in making suggestions regarding the care of your loved one.

So, my point here is to ask questions? There is nothing more tragic than a tragedy that could have been prevented. How many staff members are on during the night? What is the evacuation plan? Where does the overnight staff sleep? Can all clients be evacuated safely? You have the right to know if your loved one will be safe at all times. This can be a matter of life or death – not just for the clients living in the home but the staff as well.

Chapter Six – Medications

This is one of the most important parts of a staff member's job; the administering of medication. Agencies provide their staff with mandatory medication training. Staff must be certified to administer medication before they are allowed to administer to clients. The agency I worked for required re-certification every year through an annual course that would give us updates on medications, etc.

Staff has the responsibility to accompany the clients to their primary care physician, dentist, psychiatrist, and any other medical appointment. The right of privacy for each client is a must and must be honored. See resources in Chapter 2 on HIPPA (Medical Records).

Should an individual become ill there may be a need for a "visiting nurse" to step in and provide necessary health care. If for any reason you see an employee given the responsibility of a nurse's job, ask why? Although some staff will take on this responsibility and provide excellent care, some employees might not want the responsibility of this level of care. Most staff will not be a registered nurse nor should they try to be. Registered Nurses go through Nursing School and licensing to do what they do best.

Chapter Seven – Finances

Every client receives Social Security Income and Social Security Assistance, also known as SSI/SSA. Some families will give the company (group home) full control of their loved one's finances, but you do have the right to keep control if you so choose. That would mean you are their payee, and you would only need to send them a monthly spending check. This money can be spent on activities, needed hygiene products, clothing, and other important necessities. If you are the payee, only send your loved one what they actually need for the month. Whichever method you decide to do, make sure you keep track of their purchases. Their money could be going toward things they may not need. For example, some individuals have purchased household items like microwaves, coffee pots, outdoor grills, and even furniture for the home. This is only okay if these items are for your loved one; not for general use of the house.

To learn more about your rights, visit the Social Security Administration website:

www.ssa.gov

Chapter Eight – Meals and Nutrition

As important factor to consider is what the clients are eating. Are they being offered three healthy meals per day? Are they given choices meals?

Or some, breakfast is the most important deal of the day. Some individuals may like a good breakfast before they start their days, while others only want a cup of coffee. It is important that each individual has choices. Learn how/when breakfast is prepared; is their one seating, two seatings, or just open seating throughout a set time-frame.

Whether home for lunch where it is a prepared lunch, or a packed lunch for a client to bring with them to the day program, again options is important. Clients need to be have foods to enjoy that they like. Will the client help prepare their meal? Do they help with the selection of foods/beverages.

You can ask if the organization (group home) has hired a cook for all meal preparations or if the staff prepares the meals. Does the agency provide any training for the employees on healthy, nutritious meals? When you tour or visit the home, do you see a lot of fruits and vegetables, healthy snacks? Over the years, I have known some employees who could not cook at all; therefore, either leaving the responsibility to other employees or resorting to microwavable meals. I have also worked with employees who prepared wonderful meals for the clients and truly cared about the nutrition of everyone. Considering volunteering for a meal. The group home may permit family members to prepare a meal for all the clients; ask if this possible.

Chapter Nine – The Organization's Employees

As a caregiver in human services, there are many rewards for a staff member. The can, and most do, develop wonderful relationships with the individuals they serve. For most people in human services, the reward is intrinsic. These are the staff members who are there because they believe this is their calling and who devote their life to what they do.

You will also encounter staff that is just there for a paycheck. They may be attending college and the group home setting is perfect for them to work while affording them the flexibility to do schoolwork.

Unfortunately, there are also staff who will not pull their weight and understand the importance of all the responsibilities that come with this job. The staff are responsible for taking individuals to medical appointments, taking them shopping, assisting them with daily needs, as well as many other things. The most important task is getting the clients out in the community; helping them to become as productive as possible and integrated into society.

Staff are also responsible for the maintenance of the home. This includes cleaning, daily laundry, and meal preparation (if their isn't a dedicated cook). Their responsibilities are varied at best and at times it could become stressful and tiring to the staff. Sometimes the hours are very long; especially when the staff are doing an overnight call. Ask when relief staff arrive for the staff who have been on-call at the group home.

It is especially hard on the employees who have co-workers that are not team members and sharing the chores equally.

This leaves a huge burden on the dedicated employees who truly care. I have found that employees are often reluctant to complain about a co-worker for fear of bringing tension into the home. In most cases, there are not consequences or vey little is done to improve the bad behavior. In light of this, it would be very beneficial for you to get to know all the employees that work in the group home. By doing this, you will get to know who is truly dedicated and engaged in the care of your loved one and those who are not.

Similar to other fields of employment, there are employees that work through agencies from different countries. This is a good way for the clients and staff to learn about their countries and cultures. However, there could also be a language barrier. If you cannot understand the staff, you can't expect your loved one to. Should this happen in the home of your loved one, ask personnel or management if they provide English classes for their staff.

Chapter Ten – Quality of Life:
Community Involvement and Activities

Providing clients with a variety of opportunities is a crucial part of their development. Clients who are active in the community will have the opportunity to meet new people, and make friends. Clients afforded this opportunity are more likely to have a greater feeling of self-worth.

There are many activities that are standard in a group home, such as going to the movies, bowling, shopping, mini golfing, and going out to eat. When I worked in a group home, it was nice to see the clients go to a theatre to see a show or a stadium to attend a game of their favorite team. If you loved one is religious and attends church, it is important to request the staff honor your loved one's religious affiliation. I have heard many different excuses from staff as to why they don't bring the clients to church; however, it is their job. Should you discover your loved one hasn't been attending or even not as much as they would like, find out why. Ask the employees if there is an issue. Is the place of worship too far? Is the hour of worship not conducive to the demands of the staff's schedule. Ask, so perhaps a solution can be agreed upon. Maybe you will be in a position to help.

Many people find volunteer work as rewarding way to given back to the community. There are many organizations in need of volunteers including hospitals, nursing homes, and senior centers just to name a few.

I delivered Meals on Wheels for many years with a wonderful woman that I had the privilege of working for. She was mentally disabled and non-verbal; she had her own way communicating with facial expressions and hums. We had a special bond. Her experience with Meals on Wheels gave her great job training. If you think your loved one would benefit from some type of volunteer work, talk with the group home and discuss ways of getting him/her involved.

I will be honest and say that I was never a big believer in group activities. This is when the group home staff takes all of the clients out into the community together. I believe this brings unnecessary sometimes negative attention to the group. With one-on-one activities, just the individual and a staff member, it is a much more personable experience. However, it may not always be possible depending upon how many staff are working that day.

There are so many dedicated and caring staff members who love the individuals and develop wonderful relations over the years, but sometimes their hands are tied due to budget cuts and lack of funds. There are some organizations that expect the staff to pay for himself or herself when they take a client out for an activity. For example, if a client wanted to go to the movies or out to eat, the employee may not have the money to make that possible. This could bring a crippling consequence to the community activities. As a family member, you have the right to know if the organization provides funds for the employees to do such activities. If this is a staff member you are particularly thankful for all the care they have provided, leave them some money for such an outing. The cost of one movie is so little in the grand scheme of the amount of care they are providing.

Opening new doors, providing new and exciting experiences for all individuals who live in a group home are where they will find quality of life.

Chapter Eleven - Checklist

- ☐ Make a file of all of the individual's important paperwork.
- ☐ Get copies of all necessary documents (See Ch. 2)
- ☐ Curb Appeal – Scope out the neighborhood
- ☐ Home Safety
- ☐ List of questions you want to ask the group home
- ☐ Decide if you want to be the individual's payee and control their finances or let the agency have responsibility.
- ☐ The Staff – Did you meet a good representation of the staff?
- ☐ Is Management actively engaged with their staff and the clients?
- ☐ Move-in ready – Does home have a checklist? Consider what personal belongings to send with your loved one.

Pathways

My Brother Louis, his wife Colleen AND their son Peter, who was named after my father

③

www.ingramcontent.com/pod-product-compliance
Lightning Source LLC
Chambersburg PA
CBHW070133290526
45789CB00005B/2232